You're One Hot Diggety Dog

ILLUSTRATED BY

Suzy Spafford

Suzy's Zoo

HARVEST HOUSE PUBLISHERS

EUGENE, OREGON

You're One Hot Diggety Dog

Text Copyright © 2004 by Harvest House Publishers
Eugene, Oregon 97402

ISBN 0-7369-1415-3

Original artwork © Suzy Spafford. Wags and Whiskers™ is a trademark of Suzy's Zoo, A California Corporation.

Design and production by Garborg Design Works, Minneapolis, Minnesota

Printed in China

04 05 06 07 08 09 10 11 12 13 / LP / 10 9 8 7 6 5 4 3 2 1

To:

_____

From:

_____

You're One
Hot Diggety Dog!

You are always by my side.

Dogs have given us their absolute all. We are the center of their universe, we are the focus of their love and faith and trust.

ROGER CARAS

I can count on you to be right where I need you, when I need you.

We cannot tell the precise moment when friendship is formed. As in filling a vessel drop by drop, there is at last a drop which makes it run over; so in a series of kindnesses there is at last one which makes the heart run over.

SAMUEL JOHNSON

Don't walk in front of me,
Don't walk
Just walk beside me

Two are better than one,
because they have a good return for their work:
If one falls down,
his friend can help him up.

THE BOOK OF ECCLESIASTES

I may not follow.
behind me, I may not lead.
and be my friend.

ALBERT CAMUS

7

The moment I met you, I considered you a friend. A dear friend of the heart.

My little dog—a heartbeat at my feet.

EDITH WHARTON

Until you crossed my path, I didn't believe in kindred spirits. Now I am a true believer.

Hope deferred makes the heart sick,
but a longing fulfilled is a tree of life.

THE BOOK OF PROVERBS

*Let there be no purpose
in friendship save the
deepening of the spirit.*

KAHLIL GIBRAN

Every man passes his life

Who finds a faithful friend,
finds a treasure.

JEWISH SAYING

in the search after friendship.

RALPH WALDO EMERSON

You unselfishly love me just as I am.

A dog is the only thing on earth that loves you more than he loves himself.

JOSH BILLINGS

Your unconditional love and acceptance frees me to be myself.

I said before, that the very lives, and out of which it cannot

The friend who can be silent with us in a moment of despair or confusion, who can stay with us in an hour of grief and bereavement, who can tolerate not knowing, not curing, not healing and face with us the reality of our powerlessness, that is a friend who cares.

HENRI NOUWEN

element in which true friendship
live at all, is perfect liberty.

DINAH MARIA MULOCK CRAIK

Friendship is born at that moment when
one person says to another, "What!
You too? I thought I was the only one!"

C.S. LEWIS

Some people go to priests;

Signs on post:
DOGTOWN POP. 743
ROVER'S
K-9
DOG
DIGGITY-DOG PARK

others to poetry; I to my friends.

VIRGINIA WOOLF

17

You faithfully tend to our friendship.

There is no faith which has never yet been broken except that of a truly faithful dog.

KONRAD LORENZ

You nurture our relationship by listening, caring, and forgiving.

A Time to Talk

When a friend calls to me from the road
And slows his horse to a meaning walk,
I don't stand still and look around
On all the hills I haven't hoed,
And shout from where I am, "What is it?"
No, not as there is a time to talk.
I thrust my hoe in the mellow ground,
Blade-end up and five feet tall,
And plod: I go up to the stone wall
For a friendly visit.

ROBERT FROST

We read that we ought
but we do not read that we

The real test of friendship is:
Can you literally do nothing with the other
person? Can you enjoy together those
moments of life that are utterly simple?
They are the moments people look back
on at the end of life and
number as their most sacred experiences.

EUGENE KENNEDY

to forgive our enemies;
ought to forgive our friends.

SIR FRANCIS BACON

You're an optimist.

I think we are drawn to dogs
because they are the
uninhibited creatures
we might be if we weren't
certain we knew better.

GEORGE BIRD EVANS

I see:
A bad hair day
A road block
A mountain of work

You see:
A chance to try out a new hat
A minor change of plans
The blessing of productivity

WOOF!

Be careful the
environment you
choose for it
will shape you;
be careful the
friends you
choose for
you will become
like them.

W. CLEMENT STONE

I am wealthy in my friend

WILLIAM SHAKESPEARE

I expect to pass through this world but once; any good thing therefore that I can do, or any kindness that I can show to any fellow creature, let me do it now; let me not defer or neglect it, for I shall not pass this way again.

STEPHEN GRELLET

Whoever is happy will make others happy too.

ANNE FRANK

25

You always point me in the right direction.

Dogs are our link to paradise.
They don't know evil or jealousy
or discontent.
To sit with a dog on a hillside
on a glorious afternoon
is to be back in Eden,
where doing nothing was
not boring—it was peace.

MILAN KUNDERA

When my path is random and uncertain, you step beside me and guide me with purpose and assurance.

27

Just as yellow gold is
tested in the fire,
So is friendship to be
tested by adversity.

OVID

Life is partly what we make it,
and partly what it is made by the friends
whom we choose.

TEHYI HSIEH

Wise words pour out of her as naturally
as doubts pour out of me. Each week
I bring a problem or a scattered thought
and she listens….As a result, I have
the experience of being heard
by another person—a huge gift.

SUE BENDER

You have the courage to stand up for what you believe in.

Even the tiniest poodle is lionhearted, ready to do anything to defend home, master, and mistress.

LOUIS SABIN

Through word and deed, you make your priorities known—faith, friendship, and truth.

Friendship with oneself is all important because without it one cannot be friends with anybody else in the world.

ELEANOR ROOSEVELT

Courage is not simply one the form of every

It is not what you give your friend, but
what you are willing to give him that
determines the quality of friendship.

MARY DIXON THAYER

*It is not so
much our friends'
help that helps us
as the confident
knowledge that
they will help us.*

EPICURUS

of the virtues but
virtue at the testing point.

C.S. LEWIS

A friendly discussion
the sparks that fly

34

is as stimulating as
when iron strikes iron.

THE BOOK OF PROVERBS

You're sad when I'm sad; you're happy when I'm happy.

One reason a dog is such a comfort when you are downcast is that he doesn't ask to know why.

ANONYMOUS

When I am giddy, sad,
moody, glad...
you sit beside me and let me feel my emotion.

Friendship improves happiness and abates misery by doubling our joy and dividing our grief.

JOSEPH ADDISON

The only reward of virtue is
the only way to have a friend is

Do not assume that she who seeks to comfort you now lives untroubled among the simple and quiet words that sometimes do you good. Her life may also have much sadness and difficulty that remains far beyond yours. Were it otherwise, she would never have been able to find these words.

RAINER MARIA RILKE

virtue;
to be a friend.

RALPH WALDO EMERSON

You shake off things that don't matter.

The dog has an enviable mind;
it remembers the nice
things in life and quickly
blots out the nasty.

BARBARA WOODHOUSE

*You ignore trivial matters and focus
on what really counts…like your friends.*

41

Life is to be fortified by many friendships.
To love, and to be loved,
Is the greatest happiness of existence.

SYDNEY SMITH

Happiness is not having what you want, but wanting what you have.

RABBI H. SCHACHTEL

To be interested in the
changing seasons is a happier
state of mind than to be
hopelessly in love with spring.

GEORGE SANTAYANA

Consult your friend on all things, especially
on those which respect yourself. His
counsel may then be useful where your own
self-love might impair your judgment.

SENECA

You miss me when I am gone.

There is just something about dogs that makes you feel good. You come home, they're thrilled to see you. They're good for the ego.

JANET SCHNELLMAN

When I return home, you tell me what I missed while I was away. Your smile of welcome tells me that I was missed.

44

Friendship is the perfection of love,
and superior to love; it is love purified,
exalted, proved by experience
and a consent of minds.

SAMUEL RICHARDSON

A friend loves

One friend in a lifetime is much;
Two are many;
Three are hardly possible.

HENRY ADAMS

*The making of friends,
who are real friends,
is the best token
we have of a man's
success in life.*

EDWARD EVERETT HALE

at all times...

THE BOOK OF PROVERBS